D1443795

GREATEST FEMALE
ATHLETES
OF ALL TIME

BY TODD KORTEMEIER

MAYO
CLINIC

23

boost
mobile

WOMEN IN
SPORTS

SportsZone

An Imprint of Abdo Publishing
abdopublishing.com

abdopublishing.com

Published by Abdo Publishing, a division of ABDO, PO Box 398166, Minneapolis, Minnesota 55439. Copyright © 2018 by Abdo Consulting Group, Inc. International copyrights reserved in all countries. No part of this book may be reproduced in any form without written permission from the publisher. SportsZone™ is a trademark and logo of Abdo Publishing.

Printed in the United States of America, North Mankato, Minnesota
042017
092017

THIS BOOK CONTAINS
RECYCLED MATERIALS

Cover Photo: Jessica Hill/AP Images
Interior Photos: Jessica Hill/AP Images, 1; AP Images, 4–5; Jim Kerlin/AP Images, 6; Laurence Harris/AP Images, 8; Lennox McLendon/AP Images, 10–11; Ronald Kennedy/AP Images, 13; Eric Draper/AP Images, 15; Rick Stevens/AP Images, 16–17; Dave Caulkin/AP Images, 18; BPI/Rex Features/AP Images, 21; Jim Gund/Sports Illustrated/Getty Images, 23; Otto Greule Jr./Getty Images Sport/Getty Images, 24; Todd Warshaw/Getty Images Sport/Getty Images Karl Crutchfield/AI Wire Photo Service/Newscom, 27; Charles Dharapak/AP Images, 28–29; Jae C. Hong/AP Images, 30; Andy Brownbill/AP Images, 32; Antonio Calanni/AP Images, 34–35; Adrian Wyld/The Canadian Press/AP Images, 36; Mark Humphrey/AP Images, 38; Eugenio Savio/AP Images, 40–41; Julian Avram/Cal Sport Media/AP Images, 42; Natacha Pisarenko/AP Images, 44

Editor: Patrick Donnelly
Series Designer: Laura Polzin
Content Consultant: Rita Liberti, PhD, Professor of Kinesiology, California State University, East Bay

Publisher's Cataloging-in-Publication Data

Names: Kortemeier, Todd, author.
Title: Greatest female athletes of all time / by Todd Kortemeier.
Description: Minneapolis, MN : Abdo Publishing, 2018. | Series: Women in sports | Includes bibliographical references and index.
Identifiers: LCCN 2017930234 | ISBN 9781532111549 (lib. bdg.) | ISBN 9781680789393 (ebook)
Subjects: LCSH: Athletes--Juvenile literature. | Women athletes--Juvenile literature.
Classification: DDC 796--dc23
LC record available at http://lccn.loc.gov/2017930234

TABLE OF CONTENTS

CHAPTER 1
BABE DIDRIKSON ZAHARIAS 4

CHAPTER 2
JACKIE JOYNER-KERSEE 10

CHAPTER 3
SERENA WILLIAMS 16

CHAPTER 4
SHERYL SWOOPES 22

CHAPTER 5
RONDA ROUSEY 28

CHAPTER 6
HAYLEY WICKENHEISER 34

CHAPTER 7
MARTA 40

GLOSSARY 46
FOR MORE INFORMATION 47
INDEX 48
ABOUT THE AUTHOR 48

BABE DIDRIKSON ZAHARIAS

Growing up in Beaumont, Texas, in the 1920s, Mildred Ella "Babe" Didrikson played every sport available to girls. Sports were a huge part of her childhood: basketball, track, tennis, baseball, or anything else she got a chance to try.

Her nickname came from her Norwegian mother. She called her daughter *min bebe* in her native language. But the way Didrikson told it, her nickname was a reference to slugger Babe Ruth, because Didrikson hit so many home runs as a ballplayer. She wanted nothing less than to be the greatest athlete of all time.

Though she stood just 5 feet 5 inches tall, only a fool would underestimate her. She was amazingly strong and muscular. In a time when society expected women—even athletes—to be

Babe Didrikson, *right*, clears a hurdle at the 1932 Summer Olympics.

soft and fragile, Didrikson showed that women could be strong, tough competitors.

Didrikson was a star basketball player, but she really made a name for herself in track and field. When she was a teenager, she read about the 1928 Olympics in the newspaper and vowed that she would compete in the

Didrikson was an elite athlete who excelled in many sports, but she had the most professional success in the golf world.

Games one day. She set out to qualify for the 1932 Olympics.

Didrikson qualified in five events, but at the time, athletes weren't allowed to take part in more than three events at the Olympics. Didrikson competed in the javelin throw, 80-meter hurdles, and high jump in Los Angeles. She took the gold in the first two, setting world records in the process. She won a silver medal in the high jump.

In 1938, Didrikson decided to challenge the top male golfers in the world by playing a few events on the Professional Golfers' Associaion of America (PGA) Tour. She played in three more men's tournaments in 1945 and made the cut in all three. She is the only woman to make the cut at a PGA tournament.

Soon after, she took up golf, despite having never played the sport before. To practice her game, she hit up to 1,000 golf balls per day. Her powerful swing allowed her to drive the ball approximately 240 yards (220 meters) from the tee. Before long she became known more for golf than track and field.

After marrying professional wrestler George Zaharias in 1938, the newly named Babe Didrikson Zaharias won her first professional tournament in 1940. Over the next

ANNIKA SÖRENSTAM

In her 14-year career, Annika Sörenstam was one of the most consistently excellent golfers on the LPGA Tour. The Swedish star won 72 tournaments, the third-most of all time. Her wins included 10 majors. She won eight LPGA player of the year awards and was inducted into both the LPGA and World Golf Tour Halls of Fame, a rare achievement for an active player. Sörenstam retired in 2008 at the age of 37, still at the top of her game.

15 years, she won 41 Ladies Professional Golf Association (LPGA) Tour events, including victories in 10 major tournaments. A cancer diagnosis in 1953 did not slow her down. She missed 10 months recovering from treatment, but she came back to win the Women's US Open in 1954.

Her cancer returned in 1955. Though she continued to play on the tour, she grew weaker and died in September 1956. Four months later, she was awarded the Bob Jones Trophy for outstanding sportsmanship in golf. Despite having her career cut short, Didrikson Zaharias still is in the top 10 in all-time wins in women's golf.

Didrikson Zaharias holds the Women's British Amateur trophy after winning the event in 1947.

JACKIE
JOYNER-KERSEE

The house Jackie Joyner grew up in was modest, but it was the home of future champions. Jackie was born March 3, 1962, the second child of Mary and Alfred Joyner. Jackie's older brother, Al, became an Olympic gold medal-winning triple jumper.

When the Joyners were growing up in East St. Louis, Illinois, their neighborhood could be violent. Drug dealers operated in the open. But Jackie stayed out of trouble, got good grades, and along the way discovered track and field. By the time she was 12, she had posted a 17-foot (5.2-meter) long jump.

Joyner continued running track in high school, and she also played basketball. Those two sports brought her to the University of California, Los Angeles (UCLA). In basketball Joyner was a four-year starter at forward and

Jackie Joyner-Kersee throws the javelin during the heptathlon competition at the 1988 Summer Olympics.

even played briefly as a professional after college. But her true calling was on the track.

Joyner earned a silver medal in the heptathlon at the 1984 Summer Olympics. Her coach and future husband Bob Kersee had seen her potential in the heptathlon and worked with her on dominating that event. The heptathlon tests an athlete's skills across seven events. Competitors earn points based on their performance in each event. It's a grueling challenge. The Olympic gold medalist in the heptathlon is usually considered the greatest female athlete in the world. At the 1986 Goodwill Games, Joyner-Kersee became the first athlete ever to top 7,000 points in the heptathlon.

Joyners were everywhere at the 1988 Olympics. Fellow American track star Florence Griffith Joyner was married to Jackie's brother Al. Griffith Joyner won three gold medals in 1988, including a still-standing world record in the 100-meter dash.

Joyner-Kersee had come very close to gold in 1984. She lost by just five points and got the silver medal. She was determined not to let that happen again in 1988. In the Olympic trials that year, she broke her own world record with 7,215 points.

Joyner-Kersee clears the high jump bar, part of her record-setting performance in the 1988 Olympic heptathlon.

At the Olympics in South Korea, Joyner-Kersee was a big favorite to win gold. But she injured her knee in the high jump and fell off her world-record pace. On the second day of competition, she set an Olympic record in long jump. It all came down to the 800-meter run. She needed to finish in 2:13.67 for the world record.

ALLYSON FELIX

After bursting onto the scene at the Athens Olympics in 2004, Allyson Felix became one of the most dominant female sprinters ever. She won the silver medal that year in the 200-meter dash. Then she did it again in 2008. In 2012 Felix broke through and won the gold not only in the 200 but in the 4×100 and 4×400 relays. She tried for another gold in the 400 in 2016 but came up just short. Still, the silver medal gave Felix seven career Olympic medals, the most for any American woman in track and field.

Joyner-Kersee ran it in 2:08.51. She broke her own world record again with a score of 7,291 points. Through the 2016 Summer Olympics, nobody had come close to topping that score. In fact, Joyner-Kersee owns the top six heptathlon scores of all time.

But she still wasn't done. She won another Olympic gold in the heptathlon and added a bronze in the long jump in 1992. In Atlanta at the 1996 Games, at the age of 34, Joyner-Kersee completed her medal collection with another bronze in the long jump.

Joyner-Kersee celebrates her bronze medal in the long jump at the 1996 Olympics in Atlanta.

SERENA WILLIAMS

Growing up, Serena Williams had a familiar coach and a familiar playing partner. They were her father, Richard, and her older sister, Venus. Richard Williams wasn't a tennis expert, but he raised his daughters to be some of the best to ever play the game.

Not many kids played tennis in their hometown of Compton, California. Certainly not many black girls did. But Richard Williams never let his daughters believe there was anything they could not do. Williams could be strict with Venus and Serena, but his determination and their hard work helped them capitalize on their incredible athletic abilities.

Serena made her professional debut in 1995 at the age of 14. By 1998 she was one of the top 20 players in the world. She beat five top-10 players in her first 16 professional matches. No one had ever done that. Serena made her debut in all four Grand Slam events that year. Though Venus had a year head start, Serena was first

Serena, *right*, and Venus Williams took the tennis world by storm in the late 1990s.

to win a Grand Slam title. She took the 1999 US Open championship at the age of 17. She and Venus used to talk about which Grand Slam event they most wanted to win. While Venus said Wimbledon, Serena said winning the US Open was a dream come true.

Serena Williams stretches for a forehand in the 2002 Wimbledon women's singles final.

Serena was a revelation to the tennis world. Her powerful serve and ability to cover the court made her a fan favorite. Her forehand was deadly and her backhand strong enough that she always had a chance to return even the most difficult shots.

Serena Williams officially became the greatest tennis player in the world in 2002. She reached number one in the world rankings for the first time that summer. She won three of the four Grand Slam events in 2002, taking the French Open, Wimbledon, and the US Open. In January 2003, she added the Australian Open, meaning she held all four Grand Slam titles at once.

Serena Williams is a four-time Olympic gold medalist. Three of her medals were doubles titles with her sister Venus. Her lone singles title came in London in 2012.

Serena beat Venus in the 2003 Wimbledon final, but a knee injury and resulting surgery caused Serena to struggle for years. In 2006, she fell out of the world top 100. But in January 2007, ranked 81st, she earned a remarkable comeback win in the Australian Open final over Maria Sharapova. Williams was back.

STEFFI GRAF

From 1982 to 1999, Steffi Graf compiled one of the most dominant careers in the history of tennis. Graf spent more than seven years atop the world rankings, and from March 2, 1987, to June 8, 1997, she never fell out of the world's top two. Graf won more than 900 singles matches and 22 Grand Slam events. Shortly after retirement, she married American tennis great Andre Agassi. They were both inducted as players into the International Tennis Hall of Fame.

She regained her number one ranking in 2009 and won two more Grand Slam tournaments. At 28, she was at an age where many tennis players start to decline. But Williams seemed to get even stronger. In 2015, she nearly won all four Grand Slam events, falling just short with a loss in the US Open semifinals.

In September 2016 Williams lost the number one ranking for the first time since February 2013. But she wasn't done making history. In January 2017 she beat her sister in the finals of the Australian Open. It was Serena's 23rd Grand Slam singles title, second only to Margaret Court's 24. And at age 35, she became the oldest woman to win a Grand Slam singles title.

Williams prepares to serve at the 2016 US Open.

SHERYL SWOOPES

Sheryl Swoopes put on a show in the 1993 National Collegiate Athletic Association (NCAA) women's basketball national championship game. She scored 47 points to lift Texas Tech over Ohio State. Through 2016 no man or woman had ever scored more in a national title game.

Today, dominant college players go on to play in the Women's National Basketball Association (WNBA). But the WNBA was still four years away from existence when Swoopes's college career ended. Instead of playing professional basketball, Swoopes took a job at a bank. But she would one day help take women's basketball to the big stage.

Swoopes did find a basketball home with Team USA. She played in the 1994 Goodwill Games and the World Championships. Leading up to the 1996 Summer Olympics in Atlanta, Swoopes and Team USA played 52 warmup games against college and international teams. Swoopes

Sheryl Swoopes fights for a rebound against an Ohio State defender in the 1993 NCAA title game.

scored nearly 12 points a game as the United States went undefeated.

After helping lead the US team to Olympic gold, Swoopes joined the Houston Comets as the first player signed by a WNBA team. Already an international star, she was about to become one of professional basketball's biggest names. She even became the first woman ever to endorse her own shoe: the Nike Air Swoopes.

But Swoopes had to sit out the start of the WNBA's first season because she was pregnant with her son, Jordan. He was born four days after the league tipped off in June 1997. Swoopes missed Houston's first 19 games, but just six weeks after giving birth, she was back in action. Swoopes joined a Comets squad that was dominating the WNBA. She helped them beat the New York Liberty in the first-ever WNBA championship.

Swoopes and the Comets won the first four WNBA titles. In their final one in 2000, Swoopes led

Swoopes' son, Jordan Jackson, followed in his mom's footsteps by playing basketball at Texas Tech in 2015–16. After seeing little playing time, he transferred to Midland College for his sophomore season.

Swoopes was one of the leaders of the US team that rolled to the gold medal at the 1996 Summer Olympics.

MAYA MOORE

Maya Moore isn't used to losing. In her four years at the University of Connecticut, the Huskies went 150–4. They won 90 in a row at one point. And Moore was a big reason for their success. She scored the fourth-most points in NCAA history and won a slew of player of the year and MVP awards. She was a first overall draft pick by the WNBA's Minnesota Lynx in 2011 and kept right on winning. She led the Lynx to WNBA titles in 2011, 2013, and 2015, and she was named league MVP in 2014.

the league in points and won the first of her three WNBA Most Valuable Player (MVP) Awards. She also led Team USA to gold medals at the 2000 Olympics in Sydney, Australia, and the 2004 Games in Athens, Greece.

Swoopes played one season with the Seattle Storm in 2008 before retiring. But she couldn't stay away from the game. Swoopes made a comeback in 2011 at the age of 40, signing with the Tulsa Shock. She played in 28 of 33 games before retiring again for good. Her status as one of the greatest basketball players ever was cemented with her induction into the Naismith Memorial Basketball Hall of Fame in 2016.

Swoopes joined the WNBA's Houston Comets in 1997.

RONDA ROUSEY

Ronda Rousey is more than just a fighter. She is a highly trained martial artist. Athletic ability runs in her family. Ronda's mom, 1984 American judo champion AnnMaria De Mars, also was her first coach.

Rousey has been fighting all her life. When she was born, the umbilical cord was wrapped around her neck and she wasn't getting enough oxygen. She survived, but she had developmental problems. She wasn't able to speak until she was four years old.

Ronda discovered judo when she was 8, and by age 16 she was training for the Olympics. She worked hard but was disappointed when she placed ninth at the 2004 Games in Athens. She kept competing and ended up winning bronze at the 2008 Beijing Olympics.

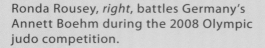

Ronda Rousey, *right*, battles Germany's Annett Boehm during the 2008 Olympic judo competition.

Her life changed forever one night while working as a bartender to pay the bills. She saw her first mixed martial arts (MMA) bout on TV.

"I could totally do that," she said to herself.

Young fighters—especially women—don't earn much money as they climb the ladder to the UFC. Before she made it big, Rousey had to work several part-time jobs to make ends meet. She was a waitress, a physical therapist for dogs, and an employee at a fitness center.

Rousey turned pro in 2011 and soon became a force in MMA. From her judo career, she borrowed a move called an armbar that was almost impossible for opponents to escape. Nine of her first 12 MMA wins came by armbar. She dominated the sport's lower divisions before signing with the Ultimate Fighting Championship (UFC) in 2012.

Her first UFC opponent didn't even make it out of the first round. That became something of a trend for anyone who tangled with "Rowdy" Ronda Rousey. Five of her first six fights in UFC ended in the first round. One lasted only 14 seconds.

Rousey, *top*, lands a punch on Liz Carmouche at UFC 157 in February 2013.

Rousey, *left*, squares off against Holly Holm in 2015.

Those six fights were all successful title defenses for Rousey. She used her quickness, strength, balance, and smarts to overwhelm her opponents. UFC President Dana White called her the greatest athlete he had ever worked with. So few expected that trend to change when she faced Holly Holm on November 14, 2015.

Rousey was an overwhelming favorite. But there was no first-round knockout on that night. Rousey was on defense from the very start. Holm wore Rousey down with her superior boxing skills. Holm even managed to slip out of Rousey's notorious armbar. In the second round, Holm aggressively went after Rousey, dropping her to the mat with a leg kick.

Rousey had to spend the night in the hospital, and her unbeaten streak was over. But after taking some time off, Rousey started training again. She promised fans that she would return, better than ever.

LAILA ALI

Laila Ali's boxing career proved that she was more than just a famous last name. While her father Muhammad Ali may have been the greatest of all time, Laila left little doubt that she was the greatest in the history of women's boxing. Ali made her pro boxing debut in 1999, knocking out April Fowler in 31 seconds. She never lost a match, finishing her career 24–0 with 21 knockouts. Not even her father could claim a perfect record.

HAYLEY WICKENHEISER

When Hayley Wickenheiser played in her first world championship in 1994, her home country of Canada had approximately 10,000 female hockey players. That number grew tenfold in the next two decades as Wickenheiser and her teammates dominated dozens more international tournaments.

Wickenheiser has as much to do with that as anybody. She was a pioneer of the sport back when there weren't even teams for girls to play on. Hayley had to prove herself playing on boys' teams. She got funny looks when she carried her hockey bag into the arena. But she excelled once she hit the ice. She skated as fast and blasted her slap shot just as hard as the rest of the players on her team.

At just 15 years old, Hayley made her debut with the Canadian Women's National Team in 1993. She soon became the captain of Team Canada and a permanent fixture in all international competitions.

Hayley Wickenheiser fires a slap shot for Team Canada.

She played at the first five Winter Olympics in which
women's hockey was an official sport. In all but one, Team
Canada won the gold medal.

Wickenheiser celebrates after leading Team Canada to the gold
medal at the 2010 Olympics in Vancouver, Canada.

JAYNA HEFFORD

Few hockey players can match Hayley Wickenheiser's achievements. But at least one can rival her longevity. Jayna Hefford was her teammate going back to 1997. Hefford also played in every Winter Olympics from 1998 to 2014 as well as 12 World Championships. She retired with the third-most points and games played for the Canadian national team. One of her greatest moments with Team Canada came when she scored the goal that won the gold medal at the 2002 Olympic Games.

Wickenheiser won just about all there is to win in international hockey. But her professional career was limited by the lack of pro women's leagues. So Wickenheiser decided to test herself by playing professional men's hockey in Europe.

In January 2003 she became the first woman ever to score a point in a men's professional league. Wickenheiser played 12 games of the 2002–03 season with Salamat in Finland, posting one goal and three assists. She played parts of two other seasons in Europe. In 2013, she became one of the first two women featured in the National Hockey League series of video games.

Wickenheiser led Canada to another gold medal at the 2014 Olympics in Sochi, Russia. The gold medal game against the United States went to overtime. In the extra period, Wickenheiser got loose for a breakaway and was hauled down by a US defender. The penalty put Canada on the power play, and Marie-Philip Poulin scored to give Canada another gold medal.

In 2000 Wickenheiser accomplished the rare achievement of becoming an Olympian at both the Summer and Winter Olympics. She was an excellent softball player and competed with Canada at the 2000 Summer Olympics.

Wickenheiser played on a broken foot during the Olympics. She had surgery soon after, casting doubt on her hockey future. Some observers speculated that Wickenheiser wanted to play in one more Olympics. But in January 2017, she announced her retirement via a tweet that said, in part, "It has been the greatest honour of my life to play for you."

Team Canada's loss, however, is the world's gain. Wickenheiser completed her master's degree in medical studies in 2015. When she announced her retirement, she said her next step would be to attend medical school.

Wickenheiser catches her breath during the overtime period of the gold-medal game at the 2014 Olympics in Russia.

MARTA

Pelé. Ronaldo. Neymar. Brazil's most legendary soccer players are known by just one name. Marta is no exception. The prolific goal scorer has had one of the most decorated soccer careers in history. In her home country, she is just as beloved as those other legends, if not more. Fans love Marta's goals, but they also respect her professionalism and humility.

Marta Vieira da Silva grew up like most Brazilian soccer stars. She played in the streets, honing her skills against the boys in her neighborhood. At 14, she tried out for a soccer club in Rio de Janeiro. She made the team, and three years later she was playing for Brazil's national team in the 2003 Women's World Cup. She scored three goals in the tournament.

Surrounded by Australian defenders, Marta looks for an open teammate during a 2016 Olympic match.

MIA HAMM

Mia Hamm was one of the world's first superstars of women's soccer. The American was a tough, hardworking player who was also kind to fans and helped promote soccer to millions of girls. She debuted with the US national team in 1987 at the age of 15 and went on to become the world's all-time leading goal scorer. She was named the best player in the world in 2000 and 2001. She won the Women's World Cup in 1991 and 1999, and she led Team USA to Olympic gold medals in 1996 and 2004. Hamm retired after the 2004 Olympics, carrying the US flag in the closing ceremony.

Marta has played much of her professional career in Sweden. She played from 2003 to 2008 with Umeå IK, helping the club win four league titles. She led the league in scoring three times and won her first World Player of the Year Award in 2006. She has also played pro soccer in the United States and Brazil.

Marta won World Player of the Year for the next four years and also was MVP of the 2007 Women's World Cup. In 2015, she scored her 15th goal at the World Cup, setting a record for the most ever.

Marta is a threat to score every time she touches the ball on the attack.

However, even though she played every minute of four Women's World Cups for Brazil, a championship has eluded her. There have been close calls. Her two goals in the semifinals in 2007 got Brazil to the final, where they lost. She scored to put Brazil on top 2–1 in 2011 against the United States, but Brazil was knocked out by penalty kicks.

Marta and Neymar both wear jersey No. 10 for Brazil. In the 2016 Olympics, when the men's team was shut out in its first two games, some Brazil fans crossed out Neymar's name on their jerseys and wrote in Marta's.

After winning her second silver medal in the Olympics on home soil in 2016, Marta set her sights to 2019. If she is able to play in a fifth World Cup, she will be guiding the next generation of players trying to bring a world championship to Brazil.

Marta's passion for the game makes her a fan favorite in Brazil and around the world.

GLOSSARY

BACKHAND
In tennis, a swing at the ball on the opposite side of the body from the athlete's dominant hand.

CUT
An elimination of players with a certain score or worse in a golf tournament after two rounds of play.

DRAFT
The process by which teams select players who are new to the league.

FOREHAND
In tennis, a swing at the ball on the same side of the body as the athlete's dominant hand.

GRAND SLAM EVENT
In tennis, one of four of the most important tournaments on the professional tour.

HURDLES
A running event in track and field in which athletes jump over obstacles in a race.

JAVELIN
A track and field event in which competitors try to throw a long stick the farthest.

JUDO
A form of martial arts in which athletes try to pin each other to the ground.

KNOCKOUT
When a fight ends by one competitor being physically unable to continue.

MAJOR TOURNAMENT
In women's golf, one of five most important tournaments on the professional tour.

SOPHOMORE
A student's second year in school.

BOOKS

Kawa, Katie. *Women in Sports.* New York: PowerKids Press, 2016.

Rutherford, Kristina. *Level the Playing Field: The Past, Present, and Future of Women's Pro Sports.* Berkeley, CA: Owlkids Books, 2016.

Stout, Glenn. *Yes, She Can! Women's Sports Pioneers.* Boston: Houghton Mifflin Harcourt, 2011.

WEBSITES

To learn more about women in sports, visit **abdobooklinks.com**. These links are routinely monitored and updated to provide the most current information available.

PLACE TO VISIT

Women's Basketball Hall of Fame
700 South Hall of Fame Drive
Knoxville, Tennessee 37915
865-633-9000
www.wbhof.com
The Women's Basketball Hall of Fame is the only one of its kind. It showcases the greatest players and people from the history of women's basketball. It also includes areas where you can test your basketball skills or see the world's largest basketball.

INDEX

Agassi, Andre, 20
Ali, Laila, 33
Ali, Muhammad, 33

Court, Margaret, 20

De Mars, AnnMaria, 28
Didrikson Zaharias,
    Babe, 4, 6–7, 9

Felix, Allyson, 14
Fowler, April, 33

Goodwill Games, 12, 22
Graf, Steffi, 20
Griffith Joyner,
    Florence, 12

Hamm, Mia, 43
Hefford, Jayna, 37
Holm, Holly, 32–33
Houston Comets, 25

Joyner-Kersee, Jackie,
    10, 12–14

Ladies Professional
    Golf Association, 9

Marta, 40, 43, 45

New York Liberty, 25
Neymar, 40, 45

Ohio State University,
    22
Olympic Games, 6–7,
    10, 12–14, 19, 22,
    25, 26, 28, 36, 37,
    39, 43, 45

Poulin, Marie-Philip, 39
Professional Golfers'
    Association of
    America, 7

Rousey, Ronda, 28,
    31–33
Ruth, Babe, 4

Seattle Storm, 26
Sharapova, Maria, 19
Sörenstam, Annika, 9
Swoopes, Sheryl, 22,
    25–26

Texas Tech University,
    22, 25
Tulsa Shock, 26

Ultimate Fighting
    Championship,
    31–33
University of California,
    Los Angeles, 10

White, Dana, 32
Wickenheiser, Hayley,
    34, 36–37, 39
Williams, Richard, 16
Williams, Serena, 16,
    18–20
Williams, Venus, 16,
    18, 19
Women's National
    Basketball
    Association, 22,
    25–26
Women's World Cup,
    40, 43, 45

ABOUT THE AUTHOR

Todd Kortemeier is a writer and editor from Minneapolis. A graduate of the University of Minnesota's School of Journalism and Mass Communication, he has written more than 25 sports books for young people.